HURRICANE OR TORNADO?

EZRA E. KNOPP

PowerKiDS press

Published in 2026 by The Rosen Publishing Group, Inc.
2544 Clinton Street, Buffalo, NY 14224

Copyright © 2026 by The Rosen Publishing Group, Inc.

All rights reserved. No part of this book may be reproduced in any form without permission in writing from the publisher, except by a reviewer.

First Edition

Editor: Greg Roza
Book Design: Michael Flynn

Photo Credits: Cover (hurricane) BEST-BACKGROUNDS/Shutterstock.com; cover (tornado) 2466402531/Shutterstock.com; p. 5 Dennis MacDonald/Shutterstock.com; p. 6 (hurricane) Drew McArthur/Shutterstock.com; p. 6 (tornado) Silverszay/Shutterstock.com; p. 7 Minerva Studio/Shutterstock.com; p. 8 https://commons.wikimedia.org/wiki/File:Allen_1980-08-08_2230Z.png; p. 9 Matt Jeppson/Shutterstock.com; p. 10 Jonah Lange/Shutterstock.com; p. 11 https://commons.wikimedia.org/wiki/File:Tip_1979-10-12_0533Z.png; p. 12 https://commons.wikimedia.org/wiki/File:1925tornado-p2o-b.jpg; p. 13 https://commons.wikimedia.org/wiki/File:Tri-State_Tornado.JPG; p. 14 https://commons.wikimedia.org/wiki/File:Tri-State_Tornado_trackmap_(PAH).jpg; p. 15 https://commons.wikimedia.org/wiki/File:John_1994_path.png; p. 16 Capturing Adventure/Shutterstock.com; p. 17 https://commons.wikimedia.org/wiki/File:Tornado_Alley_Diagram.svg; p. 18 Zinaida Shevchuk/Shutterstock.com; p. 19 BD Images/Shutterstock.com.

Cataloging-in-Publication Data

Names: Knopp, Ezra E.
Title: Hurricane or tornado? / Ezra E. Knopp.
Description: Buffalo, New York : PowerKids Press, 2026. | Series: Fact finders: know the difference! | Includes glossary and index.
Identifiers: ISBN 9781499452754 (pbk.) | ISBN 9781499452761 (library bound) | ISBN 9781499452778 (ebook)
Subjects: LCSH: Hurricanes–Juvenile literature. | Tornadoes–Juvenile literature.
Classification: LCC QC944.2 K56 2026 | DDC 363.34'922–dc23

Manufactured in the United States of America

Some of the images in this book illustrate individuals who are models. The depictions do not imply actual situations or events.

CPSIA Compliance Information: Batch #CSPK26. For Further Information contact Rosen Publishing at 1-800-237-9932.

CONTENTS

WILD WINDS! 4

BY LAND OR BY SEA? 6

WHICH HAS FASTER WINDS? 8

BIG, BIGGER, BIGGEST 10

DEADLY WINDS. 12

TIME WILL TELL!. 14

'TIS THE SEASON!. 16

PREDICTING STORMS 18

STORM STRENGTH 20

GLOSSARY 22

FOR MORE INFORMATION 23

INDEX 24

WILD WINDS!

Earth is home to some really wild weather! Natural **disasters** are hard to **predict** and can cause millions of dollars in damage to communities across the globe. Hurricanes and tornadoes are two types of natural disaster that share things in common. Both include swirling (spinning), high-speed winds. They both often result in death and **destruction**.

But these two weather **phenomena** are very different from each other. Using a scientific approach, we can observe hurricanes and tornadoes to learn more about both.

IT CAN BE VERY DIFFICULT, OR IMPOSSIBLE, TO CORRECTLY PREDICT WHERE AND WHEN A HURRICANE OR TORNADO WILL OCCUR. METEOROLOGISTS ARE TRAINED TO USE SCIENCE TO HELP PEOPLE AVOID DANGER BY MAKING EDUCATED WEATHER PREDICTIONS.

BY LAND OR BY SEA?

Hurricanes and tornadoes have some things in common, but they are very different weather phenomena. For example, one only forms over the ocean, and the other almost always forms over land. Which is which?

WATERSPOUTS ARE TORNADOES THAT FORM OVER WATER, OR MOVE OUT OVER WATER. THEY ARE FAR WEAKER THAN LAND-BASED TORNADOES, BUT CAN BE DANGEROUS TO BOATS AND AIRCRAFT.

Hurricanes form over ocean waters that are at least 80 degrees Fahrenheit (26.7 degrees Celsius). That's why they form closer to Earth's **equator**. Tornadoes form over land when warm, wet air meets cold, dry air. This results in swirling winds and **wind shears**. Tornadoes usually form from powerful thunderstorms called supercells.

WHICH HAS FASTER WINDS?

Hurricanes and tornadoes both create fast, dangerous winds that can cause great damage. In 1980, it's believed that Hurricane Allen set a hurricane wind-speed record of 190 miles (306 km) per hour. Other hurricanes have reached a wind speed of 150 miles (241 km) per hour.

HURRICANE ALLEN

A TORNADO'S WINDS ARE SO FAST THAT THEY CAN RIP TREES OUT OF THE GROUND AND THROW THEM AS IF THEY WERE MADE OF PAPER!

Many tornados reach wind speeds over 300 miles (483 km) per hour! That's powerful enough to pick up and throw cars and tear down brick buildings. This is one reason tornadoes are so dangerous.

BIG, BIGGER, BIGGEST

High winds make both hurricanes and tornadoes dangerous, but so does the size of the weather event. Which is larger, a hurricane or a tornado?

THE WIDEST HURRICANE ON RECORD, TYPHOON TIP, HIT JAPAN IN 1979. (TYPHOON IS ANOTHER WORD FOR HURRICANE.) AT IT'S LARGEST, TIP MEASURED ABOUT 1,380 MILES (2,220 KM) WIDE. IT WOULD HAVE COVERED THE WESTERN HALF OF THE UNITED STATES!

A hurricane is much larger than a tornado. Most tornadoes are tall and thin and can leave a path of destruction 10 to 20 miles (16 to 32 km) long. Most hurricanes, however, are about 300 miles (483 km) wide! Hurricanes have a calm, clear spot in the very middle called the eye, which can be about 30 miles (48 km) wide.

DEADLY WINDS

Scientists have been studying hurricanes and tornadoes for a long time. This helps us prepare for them. According to the records, which natural disaster has resulted in more death and destruction, tornadoes or hurricanes?

GRIFFIN, INDIANA
TRI-STATE TORNADO DAMAGE

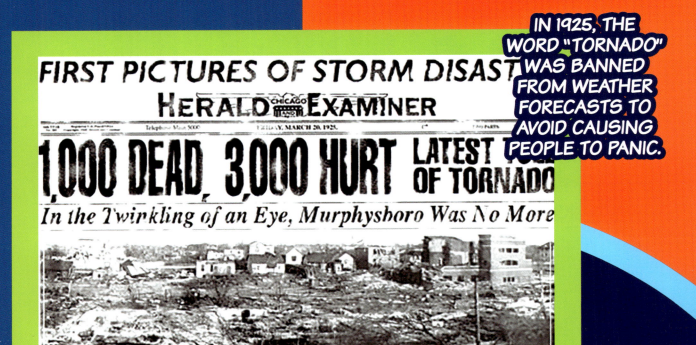

IN 1925, THE WORD "TORNADO" WAS BANNED FROM WEATHER FORECASTS TO AVOID CAUSING PEOPLE TO PANIC.

On March 18, 1925, the Tri-State Tornado killed 695 people as it moved more than 300 miles (483 km) through Missouri, Illinois, and Indiana. However, hurricanes are far more deadly. On November 12, 1970, the Bhola Cyclone (another word for hurricane) hit Bangladesh. Between 300,000 and 500,000 people died, making it one of the deadliest natural disasters on record.

TIME WILL TELL!

Which natural disaster do you think lasts longer, a hurricane or a tornado? The Tri-State Tornado of 1925 formed at 1:00 p.m. in Ellington, Missouri. It **dissipated** at 4:30 p.m. near Petersburg, Indiana. The twister (another name for a tornado) lasted 3.5 hours!

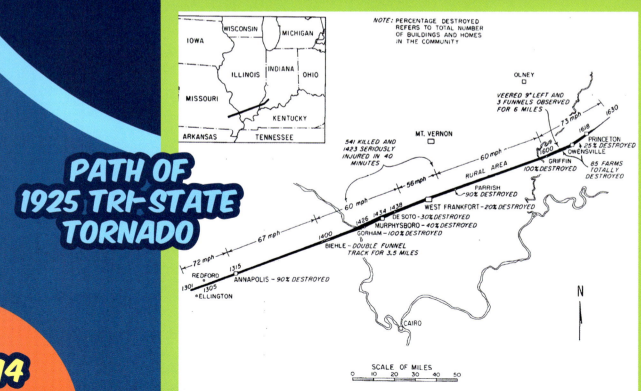

PATH OF 1925 TRI-STATE TORNADO

On August 11, 1994, Hurricane John formed in the Pacific Ocean near Central America. It traveled south of Hawaii, and then into the north Pacific. Hurricane John was active for 31 days! It dissipated on September 10.

'TIS THE SEASON!

Tornado season in the United States is generally from April to June. Hurricane season for the United States is from June to November. Which do you think there are more of during a season, tornadoes or hurricanes?

16

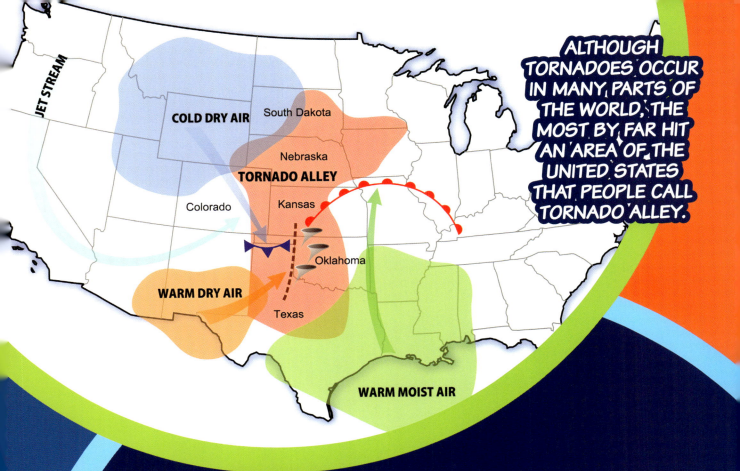

ALTHOUGH TORNADOES OCCUR IN MANY PARTS OF THE WORLD, THE MOST BY FAR HIT AN AREA OF THE UNITED STATES THAT PEOPLE CALL TORNADO ALLEY.

Each year, an average of 14 named **tropical storms** form in the Atlantic Ocean, but only a few make landfall in the United States. However, about 1,200 tornadoes hit the U.S. every tornado season! Tornadoes rarely get names, unless they have a big affect on a lot of people.

PREDICTING STORMS

Since both hurricanes and tornadoes are such destructive forces, meteorologists work hard to predict when and where these natural disasters will hit. Which do you think is easier to predict?

PREDICTED PATH OF HURRICANE MILTON (2024)

SOME SCIENTISTS EXCITEDLY GET UP CLOSE TO TORNADOES IN ORDER TO STUDY THEM. "STORM CHASERS" USE MODERN **TECHNOLOGY** TO STUDY TORNADOES, AND HEAVY TRUCKS TO STAY AS SAFE AS POSSIBLE.

Hurricanes form slowly, sometimes taking many days. They are far easier to predict. The fact that tornadoes can appear and disappear so quickly makes them very hard to predict. Meteorologists know that tornadoes happen at certain times of the year and in certain places. Still, it can be hard to say exactly where and when one may appear.

STORM STRENGTH

Meteorologists have scales that tell how strong a hurricane or tornado is. These scales let us compare and contrast information. This is an important part of scientific observation. When reading news about natural disasters, these scales can help you understand them better.

We've learned a lot about hurricanes and tornadoes, but there's so much more to learn! It's wise for us to learn all we can about natural disasters, especially if you live in an area like Tornado Alley. But it also makes you a stronger fact finder!

YOU MIGHT NOT BE FAMILIAR WITH SOME OF THE WORDS USED IN THESE SCALES TO DESCRIBE DAMAGE. HOWEVER, YOU HAVE ENOUGH INFORMATION TO FIGURE THEM OUT. IF YOU'RE STILL UNSURE, DO SOME RESEARCH (LIKE A SCIENTIST) AND FIND OUT WHAT THEY MEAN!

ENHANCED FUJITA TORNADO SCALE

EF RATING	WIND SPEED (MPH / KPH)	DAMAGE
0	65–85 / 105–137	LIGHT
1	86–110 / 138–177	MODERATE
2	111–135 / 178–217	CONSIDERABLE
3	136–165 / 218–266	SEVERE
4	166–200 / 267–322	DEVASTATING
5	HIGHER THAN 200 / 322	INCREDIBLE

SAFIR-SIMPSON HURRICANE SCALE

SS RATING	WIND SPEED (MPH / KPH)	DAMAGE
1	74–95 / 119–153	MINIMAL
2	96–110 / 154–177	MODERATE
3	111–130 / 178–209	EXTENSIVE
4	131–155 / 210–249	EXTREME
5	HIGHER THAN 155 / 249	CATASTROPHIC

GLOSSARY

destruction: The state or action of being completely ruined.

disaster: Something that happens suddenly and causes much suffering and loss for many people.

dissipate: To weaken or separate into parts before disappearing completely.

equator: An imaginary circle around Earth that's an equal distance from the North Pole and the South Pole.

phenomenon: A fact or an event that is observed.

predict: To make an educated guess about the outcome of something.

tropical storm: A swirling storm in an area of Earth that is warm and wet and which can grow into a hurricane.

technology: A method that uses science to solve problems and the tools used to solve those problems.

wind shear: An abrupt shift in wind speed and direction that occurs over a very short distance.

FOR MORE INFORMATION

BOOKS

Bolte, Mari. *Super Surprising Trivia about Natural Disasters*. North Mankato, MN: Capstone, 2024.

Crane, Cody. *All About Hurricanes*. New York, NY: Scholastic, 2021.

Crane, Cody. *All About Tornadoes*. New York, NY: Scholastic, 2021.

WEBSITES

Hurricanes
kids.nationalgeographic.com/science/article/hurricane
Discover more facts about hurricanes from National Geographic Kids.

Tornado Facts for Kids
www.coolkidfacts.com/tornado-facts-for-kids/
Read more about tornadoes from this detailed website.

Publisher's note to educators and parents: Our editors have carefully reviewed these websites to ensure that they are suitable for students. Many websites change frequently, however, and we cannot guarantee that a site's future contents will continue to meet our high standards of quality and educational value. Be advised that students should be closely supervised whenever they access the internet.

INDEX

B

Bhola Cyclone, 13

H

Hurricane Allen, 8
hurricane eye, 11
Hurricane John, 15

M

meteorologist, 5, 8, 19, 20

N

natural disaster, 4, 12, 13, 14,
    18, 20

P

predicting, 4, 5, 18, 19

S

scales, 20, 21
size, 10, 11
supercells, 7

T

Tri-State Tornado, 12, 13, 14
tropical storm, 17
Tornado Alley, 17, 20
Typhoon Tip, 11

W

waterspouts, 7
wind speed, 8, 9, 21